San Francisco Invites the World

San Francisco Invites the World

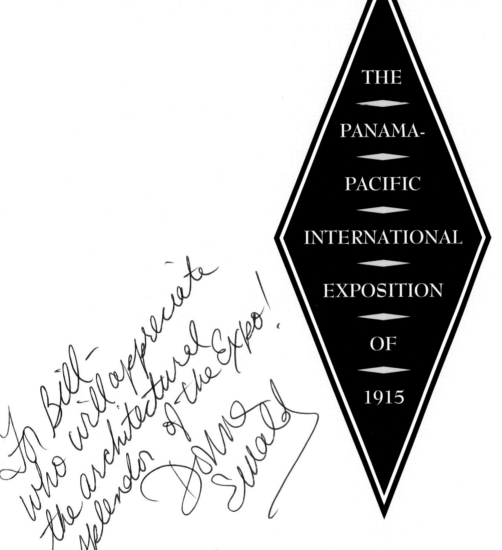

THE

PANAMA-

PACIFIC

INTERNATIONAL

EXPOSITION

OF

1915

To Bill—
who will appreciate
the architectural Expo!
splendor of the Expo!
Donna Ewald

by **DONNA EWALD** and **PETER CLUTE**

foreword by **HERB CAEN**

CHRONICLE BOOKS   SAN FRANCISCO

For my parents,
Don and Helen Ewald

— *D.E.*

In memory of
my daughter Aphra

— *P.C.*

ACKNOWLEDGMENTS

The photographs in this book are from the collections of the authors and from the collection of Vic Reyna and Ed Rogers of San Francisco. We gratefully acknowledge their contribution.

We also wish to thank Sharon Deveaux, of Deveaux Photographics, Corte Madera, for making the photographs come alive through her print and restoration work, John Sullivan, Dennis Gallagher and the staff of Visual Strategies, Annie Barrows of Chronicle Books and artist Bud Luckey for his accurate and charming map. And a very special thank-you also goes to:

Herb Caen
Jim Soladay
Umberto Tosi

Printed in Hong Kong.

ISBN: 0-87701-838-3

Library of Congress Cataloging in Publication Data.

Ewald, Donna.
San Francisco invites the world: the Panama-Pacific exposition of 1915 / by Donna Ewald and Peter Clute; foreword by Herb Caen.
p. cm.
ISBN 0-87701-838-3
1. Panama-Pacific International Exposition (1915 : San Francisco, Calif. I. Clute, Peter. II. Title.
TC781.C1E93 1991
907.4'794'61 — dc20   91-8754
                                   CIP

Book and cover design:
Visual Strategies, San Francisco

Distributed in Canada by
Raincoast Books,
112 East Third Avenue,
Vancouver, B.C. V5T 1C8

10 9 8 7 6 5 4 3 2 1

Chronicle Books
275 Fifth Street
San Francisco, California 94103

Contents

The city would never be so young again, or so bright, so fun loving, so full of self-confidence. The lights were going out all over Europe, and the rest of the world was fearful of being drawn into a raging war, but in brash San Francisco, all was brightness, music, and dancing across the hills.

It was the strange year of 1915, and San Francisco was going about the joyous experience of putting on an international exposition of such grandeur, imagination, and irresistible charm that those who attended it would have their lives changed forever.

Nobody who experienced the Panama-Pacific International Exposi-

tion will ever forget it. There are those who claim it was the finest world's fair ever put on, both for design and content. Its incredible spell is felt to this day among those who respond to great and slightly mad projects that are carried off with unrivaled panache.

"The '15 Fair," as it is spoken of with reverence, was a gamble that turned into a dazzling success, built on land dredged from San Francisco Bay. Only nine years after a devastating earthquake—one of the worst in history—San Francisco was out to show the world that it had bounced back. It did so in the way it knew best: with zest, extravagance, and buildings bursting with pride and magnificent design.

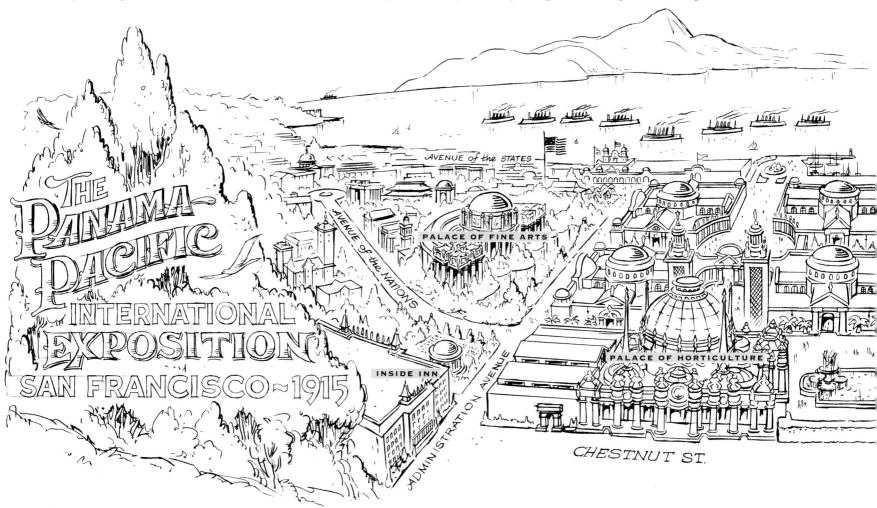

The world came to marvel at the magic city, crowned by its Tower of Jewels, that rose on the shores of the bay. Looking at the photographs today, people still marvel that the citizens of this small city could have created such splendor in so short a time. It may have been the last effusion of the "Can Do!" spirit that suffused San Francisco in its last era of innocence, high energy, and just plain guts. San Francisco was as fearless in '15 as it had been in '06.

And when the lights of the Tower of Jewels went out for the last time, the world mourned the end of a bright and shining moment. The merry-go-round turned no longer, the music faded away, and the laughing stopped.

Among the many who have been captivated and even obsessed all their lives by the legendary '15 Fair is Donna Ewald of San Francisco, who has perhaps the finest collection of photographs, memorabilia, and souvenirs of the remarkable event. For this book, she and her friend Peter Clute have put the pictures together in a way that leads you seductively and happily into the past, back to 1915, back to the entrance, back to a long tour through a short-lived miracle whose fascination has never ended.

It is a trip well worth taking, and there is no better guide to the wonder of it all.

ABOVE

An interior view of the Merchants' Exchange Building on
April 28, 1910. A meeting was held to receive and
announce subscriptions to the five-million-dollar fund that
was to be raised locally before government aid for the fair
could be obtained. C.C. Moore, chairman of the Finance
Committee, presided, and Lawrence Harris, who wrote the
poem "The Damndest Finest Ruins Ever Gazed On
Anywhere," was the auctioneer. This tremendously
successful event raised $4,089,000.

The Lost City of Domes

In 1904, Reuben Hale, a San Francisco mercantile tycoon, proposed to his fellow directors of the Merchants' Association that the city hold an exposition to celebrate the opening of the Panama Canal. The suggestion displayed the frontier bravado characteristic of a still-young, turn-of-the-century San Francisco, for it was then by no means certain that the Canal could be completed successfully.

United States Army engineers had started excavating an audaciously planned fifty-mile cut across the steamy Panamanian isthmus on May 4 of that year, attempting, where others had failed, the greatest construction project of that era. In the context of *la belle époque*, building the Panama Canal would test courage and technology as much as did sending men to the moon in our own times. Moreover, the project would take roughly the same number of years and, like the moon shot, would be undertaken with many formidable technical problems yet to be overcome. This would be construction on an enormous scale, and the project was referred to at the time in the press as the "Thirteenth Labor of Hercules." To prevail, the Americans would spend a decade digging through two mountain passes, dredging mosquito-infested swamps, and constructing locks of then-unprecedented size and lift.

The Canal would realize a dream that began four hundred years earlier. Spanish conquistadors founded Panama City in 1519, while using the isthmus as a land bridge between their home-bound Atlantic galleons and their Pacific ships hauling plundered Inca gold from the west coast of Peru. As world commerce grew in the industrial era, the French, triumphant from their building of the Suez Canal in 1869, made the first large-scale attempt at building a Panama Canal in the 1880s, but they were turned back by yellow fever and malaria. It took the Americans to discover that mosquitoes carried the fever and then to figure out how to get rid of them. And it took gunboat diplomacy to goad the Panamanian

province into breaking away from an unfriendly Colombia and forming a banana republic. The new country was then persuaded into a sweetheart deal with the bully-brash United States of Teddy Roosevelt and William Howard Taft.

The stakes were high. The Canal would forever change the geography of the Americas and, with it, world history, politics, and economics. It would link Pacific and Atlantic, the American east and west coasts, Europe and Asia. Together with the Suez Canal, it would make industrial trade on a world scale feasible and open the way to the global economy in which we now live.

Most significantly for Hale's city by the Golden Gate, the Canal would shorten the steaming distance from San Francisco to New York by 7,873 miles, to New Orleans by 8,868 miles, and to Liverpool by 5,666 miles. San Francisco—the Gold Rush town, the Jewel of the West, the Paris of the Pacific—would realize her destiny, the silver-and-railroad-baron aristocracy heralded from their Nob Hill aeries. It is not surprising that Hale's proposal, visionary though it was, was well received.

Neither was the profit potential lost on Hale and his fellow Merchants' Association colleagues. Hale himself was an owner of Hale Brothers Department Store on Market and Fifth streets. At the city's urging, a bill was introduced in the United States Congress to provide $5 million in seed money for the Exposition.

Despite such hopeful beginnings, Hale's dream soon drifted into limbo. The seed money bill stalled in Congress. Little else happened for the next year.

Then, on the morning of April 18, 1906, the Great Earthquake and the ensuing fire razed the city. Hale's department store was left a smoking ruin, along with the rest of Market Street. His proposal seemed buried with it. Hundreds were dead, thousands injured, tens of thousands homeless. Engineers surveyed the holocaust and some predicted it could take as long as twenty-five years to restore the city.

But not Hale. He and a group of business associates met that December in a shack on what had been the site of the Hotel St. Francis and revived the dream—and maybe much of the hope of San Francisco with it. They formed the Pacific Exposition Company.

Three years later, the city held a week-long festival, the Portola. It was a smashing success and showed San Franciscans that their city was well on its way not only to recovery but also to a fresh start. For the Great Earthquake and Fire, tragic though it was, also was seen as having provided the city with an opportunity to leave behind the mistakes of the past, including the rampant corruption of the old political order.

Dreamers and builders alike came forward with utopian plans for rebuilding the city. "Most of these bright schemes were forgotten," writes one historian of the day, "but not Hale's." San Francisco continued to rebuild, as newspaper dispatches reported progress in the building of the great Canal in Panama. Their destinies seemed linked. Hale's proposal became the city's vision.

Hale had no trouble rallying financial support for his idea now. Soon a committee of business leaders formed the directorate of a new corporation that was to carry forth the project on an international scale: the Panama Pacific Exposition Company. It quickly raised enough cash for the state and federal governments to take notice. There were scores of individual subscriptions of $25,000 each, as well as big company subscriptions. Another $5 million, including $250,000 from the Southern Pacific Corporation, was raised at a mass meeting held in the Merchants' Exchange Building.

The State of California responded by levying a $5 million tax fund for the project. Counties were authorized to levy their own taxes for participation. The city of San Francisco voted a bond issue for the same amount.

Getting federal support proved a little more difficult. By this time Washington, D.C., itself, along with Baltimore, Boston, and New Orleans, was wooing Congress to dub it the official Panama exposition city. New Orleans proved the most formidable competitor. But San Francisco's obvious appeal as the West Coast port of call for ships that would be passing through the Canal won the day.

On February 15, 1911, President William Howard Taft signed a resolution designating San Francisco as the Exposition site. The city went wild when the news dispatches were wired west. On October 14, Taft came to the city and turned the first spadeful of dirt to break ground for the Exposition. (This ceremony took place in Golden Gate Park, as the ultimate location of the fair had not yet been selected.) The next day, Taft lunched at the Cliff House and toasted San Francisco as "the city that knows how," thus immortalizing its sobriquet. On February 2 of the following year, Taft issued a proclamation in Washington inviting all nations to participate in what would become, in every sense, the Panama-Pacific International Exposition.

San Francisco now was on world stage center. This was an era of grand international expositions and fairs in the United States, which had started with celebrations of the American centennial in 1876 and continued through the turn of the century. Great exhibitions in Paris, Chicago, and St. Louis had displayed the power of the machine age and the wonders of a dawning modernism. Well-attended and publicized, these fairs were etched in the public consciousness of the day.

This was not lost on San Franciscans, who, having won the right to put on the Exposition, committed themselves to making it the best ever held. The Panama Exposition Company was transformed from a largely fund-raising, promotional enterprise into an organization that could carry out the challenges of designing, building, and running a fair to show the world that San Francisco truly had risen from the ashes.

A board of directors recruited from among the city's most powerful men undertook the job, all serving without pay. Among them were names still familiar today: Hale, William H. Crocker, San Francisco Chronicle founder M. H. de Young, and Mayor James Rolph, Jr., serving as vice presidents. C.C. Moore, a prominent San Francisco businessman, agreed to serve as president.

After considering several sites, the directors chose one lying largely in what then was an outlying city area called Harbor View—later to be known as the Marina District. The Exposition would cover 635 acres, including adjacent parts of the Presidio and a section of Bay lagoon and marshland extending along the Harbor View waterfront. The lagoon and ponds would be filled in and eventually would become a large part of the Marina's residential area.

Harbor View was an ideal site in that it afforded a magnificent vista of the Bay, direct transport of building materials by water, and accessibility to the city's inhabitants. But there were legal and engineering complications to overcome. The Exposition Company had to buy or lease 76 city blocks containing 200 parcels of land from 175 individual owners and tear down or move 200 buildings. It also had to acquire the United States Army's permission to use Presidio land; get help from the Army Corps of Engineers to fill the marshlands and the Harbor View cove, which was under ten to twenty feet of water, with thousands of tons of sand; and build an elaborate sewer system for the grounds. This took about six months, and it was only the beginning.

The greatest challenge was to create an overall design that would work toward several purposes. The Exposition had to accommodate varied and multiple structures and exhibits and thousands of visitors; it had to be functional and impressive; and, most important, it would have to harmonize with the natural beauty of its Bay-side setting. Great mechanical exhibits and feats of engineering were among the most memorable displays of the major expositions of that day, epitomized by the Eiffel Tower, which was erected in 1889 to celebrate the centennial of the French Revolution. But the Panama Exposition sponsors wanted no such massive ironworks by the Bay.

It was a formidable design challenge, and the directors assembled the country's best architects, designers, artists, and engineers to meet it. Moore called for a meeting of the San Francisco chapter of the American Institute of Architects for recommendations. George W. Kelham was chosen as chief of architecture. He was a San Franciscan with an aesthetic sense of place combined with the political instincts to make a great project work. Kelham had studied in Paris with the era's leading architectural lights and, as a young man, had taken part in the building of the great Paris Exhibition of 1900. Two of his most famous buildings still stand in the city: the Palace Hotel and the Bohemian Club. From the start, the architects of the Exposition realized that, vast as the Exposition was to be, and representing as it would so many disparate historical and cultural styles, the whole effect had to be one of unity.

Kelham and the architectural council under him came up with an elegantly simple plan. It would group eight main exhibition palaces together in a single block. This main block would be flanked on the eastern end by what would be the Palace of Machinery—a building nearly a thousand feet long, 367 feet wide, and 136 feet high, wherein life-sized electrical and industrial plants were to be exhibited in operation—and on the western end by the Palace of Fine Arts, Bernard Maybeck's neo-classic fantasy monument, wherein would be exhibited thousands of paintings of every style and period. (The building was restored and reinforced in the 1960s and is the only one of the Exposition's monuments that survives on the site.)

William B. Faville, another local architect, designed exterior walls surrounding the block to reflect classic eras of architectural design, with a unifying design that would contain the variety of styles. Altogether, it was a plan unprecedented and, to this day, unequaled in world expositions.

This grouping would be crowned by an Italianate main tower, which came to be known as the Tower of Jewels. The great single block of buildings would be divided by one longitudinal and three lateral streets that would intersect into magnificent courts: the Court of the Universe, the Court of Abundance, and the Court of the Four Seasons. Set in what would be the South Gardens flanking the main exhibition block of buildings would be two of what were to become the Exposition's most fantastic buildings: the Festival Hall, which seated thirty-five hundred, and the Horticulture Palace, whose soaring glass dome was the largest of its kind, bigger than the main dome of St. Peter's Basilica in Rome.

The monumental exhibition palaces would form a core that would hold together two outer zones of the Exposition, each very different from the other. At the western end, beyond the Palace of Fine Arts, would be exhibition buildings set up by participating countries, and another area for state exhibits. This included a large tract (where the Marina Green adjacent to the St. Francis Yacht Club now is located) for the mission-style California Building, which was to house exhibits from various counties.

At the opposite, eastern end of the central exhibit cluster, beyond the Palace of Machinery, would be a sixty-five-acre amusement and concessions district called the Zone. This, once the Exposition was underway, turned out to be more than an amusement park. Large-scale dioramas and other exhibits included enormous models of the Grand Canyon and Yellowstone Park, Japan Beautiful, the Creation, an "infant incubators" exhibit, and a working model of the Panama Canal.

In the end, the building of the entire fair would cost $15 million. Its construction progressed with almost uncanny smoothness, helped by

Water, by Frank Brangwyn. The four murals that made up the series *Earth, Air, Fire, and Water* are now in the Herbst Theatre of the Veterans War Memorial Building in San Francisco.

cooperation from labor leaders, and the fair opened exactly on time. Through its 288 days of existence, the fair earned enough profit to pay for the construction of San Francisco's Civic Auditorium—which was in use during the Exposition and which still stands—and to generate another $1 million surplus.

The fair's layout provided a fabulous setting for what was to become an enormous work not only of architecture but also of art and imagination. The colors, materials, and lighting used in the buildings were important aspects of the designs, and, fortuitously, talents equal to these tasks stepped forward.

Elegant landscaping with imposing hedges; more than thirty thousand cypress, acacia, spruce, eucalyptus, and other trees; and innumerable plants and flowers provided a setting that rivaled the royal gardens of Europe. All of this was at the hand of master landscape artist John McLaren, who had designed Golden Gate Park. More than fifteen hundred sculptures commissioned from artists all over the world—including a young Beniamino Bufano—stood on arches and columns, in niches, in fountains, and in free-standing groups. "They sing in many themes, always in harmony, but with no loss of character of individuality," proclaimed the Exposition's acting chief of sculpture, A. Stirling Calder.

Jules Guerin, a colorist, painter, and designer who had worked in Europe and the Middle East, oversaw the Exposition's color schemes. A specially blended plaster material in the hues of old ivory closely mimicked the travertine marble used in ancient Rome and was applied over almost all the buildings, statues, and walls. Eight accent colors were used throughout the Exposition: a French green for garden lattices, a deep cerulean blue in recessed panels and ceiling vaults, pink-orange for flagpoles, pinkish-red flecked with brown for the background of colonnades, a golden burnt-orange for moldings and small domes, terra-cotta for other domes, gold for statuary, and an antique green for urns and vases. Everything from the tiniest blade of grass to the tallest flagpole, from every flower, shrub, and tree to each statue and building conformed to this color scheme.

The crowning effect was achieved by elaborate and powerful lighting designed by W. D'Arcy Ryan, called "the Aladdin of the 1915 City Luminous." He was loaned to the Exposition by a young General Electric company eager to promote the miracles of its technology. The massive exhibition area was entirely illuminated by indirect lighting, and the huge Scintillator, a battery of searchlights on a barge in the Bay, created auroralike effects overhead. Multicolored lights played on the Tower of Jewels, and colored steam and smoke added to the pyrotechnics.

It was Ryan who also came up with what perhaps was the most exquisite and dazzling feature of the fair, the 102,000 pieces of multicolored cut Bohemian glass that glittered from the Tower of Jewels, refracting and reflecting sunlight and nighttime illumination.

In less inspired or talented hands, these juxtaposed elements might have conspired to garishness. Instead, a subtle evanescence was achieved, a mystical, dreamlike transcendence of the commonplace. Such were the impressions of the great majority of the 18 million people who attended the fair. Mingling in the crowds were workers, artists, actors, scientists: the famous and obscure. All were equally enthralled. And what they remembered was consistent. What they expressed, over and over, was a sense of wonder.

As visitors streamed through this phantasmagoric creation, it grew legendary. The Great War's carnage in Europe seemed as far from the fair as did the more innocent turn-of-the-century years that had given birth to the Exposition. America would not join the war until 1917, and the Exposition's sponsors made efforts to see that exhibitions from France and Germany went on as planned.

A magic almost beyond belief arose from the commonplace and artful details of the fair as much as from the monuments. "We saw shining, almost imaginary buildings full of unbelievable works of sculpture, painting, weaving, basketmaking, products of agriculture, and all kinds of mechanical inventions," author William Saroyan wrote of his childhood visit to the fair. It was, he thought, "a place that couldn't possibly be real."

But it was very real. Even though the Exposition closed forever on December 4, 1915, and nearly all of its buildings were demolished or moved, it remains a part of San Francisco's enduring spirit. The fair's presence can be felt even today in a setting whose basic landscape has changed only superficially. If you climb Russian Hill or stand at Broadway and Divisadero Street looking out over the Marina District, a little squinting and some imagination will blur out the Golden Gate Bridge and other modern features, and, with the Palace of Fine Arts as a focal point, the old Exposition will glimmer into view.

The Exposition has been real for me for almost as long as I can remember. My mother's parents courted at the fair, and I remember them relating tidbits about famous and infamous characters spotted there: seeing Fatty Arbuckle and Mabel Normand walking in the Zone, hearing Billy Sunday preach and William Jennings Bryan exhort the masses.

I was curious to see and hear more about this magical place. Following the example of my parents, who love to collect things, I began collecting whatever I could find that had been connected with the fair. Once, in a tiny, cluttered antiques store in the Gold Country, I discovered a trove of the pieces of Bohemian cut glass that had adorned the Tower of Jewels. The owner of the shop had no idea what these lovely crystals were, but I knew them at once. Over the years, in dusty antiques stores, garage sales, and flea markets I acquired souvenir spoons, trophies, paperweights, silk scarves, paintings, postcards, etchings, badges, ribbons, pennants, photos—altogether a collection of more than four thousand items that brings the fair back to life.

This fascination melded with a love of San Francisco's turn-of-the-century halcyon days, a tumultuous and romantic era. And following this fascination led me to others who share it. I was lucky enough to meet Peter Clute, the great New Orleans jazz piano player and a partner in Earthquake McGoon's, home of Turk Murphy's Jazz Band. Pete and I shared many forays to junk shops and antiques fairs. This book realizes a dream we also share, to somehow re-create the fair for others as vividly as it lives in our imaginations.

The fair was much more than its buildings, magnificent though they were. The sum of this event was in the loving details, its gardens and courts, its attractions, its art, and its oddities. This book is a lovingly lingering tour of sights chosen from a collection of photographs taken at the time of the Exposition.

Come with us to the fair. It's right this way, down Scott Street, through McLaren's hedge—through the looking glass.

CHAPTER ONE

The Beginning

The construction of
the fairgrounds, from the
first spadeful of earth
to the opening festivities.

The Fulton Iron Works at Harbor View. The ironworks sold its buildings to the Exposition Company because they were too difficult to move. They were torn down.

Work begins at Harbor View. In March 1912, the San Francisco Bridge Company was awarded the first contract for filling the cove, which was enclosed by a seawall running east and west along the boundary of the fairgrounds. The hydraulic line put 300,000 cubic yards of fill in the area, on top of which buildings were constructed. Here you can see the future site of Hawaii's building next to Utah's site (indicated by the signs). Most of the damage in the 1989 earthquake was in the former cove area of Divisadero to Fillmore, and Bay to the water's edge.

Sale property on the Exposition site. More than 76 city blocks were cleared or filled. The Exposition Company bought or leased the land and then sold any existing buildings. Those not salable were razed.

On Thanksgiving Day 1912, a large procession of San Franciscans escorts a petition to bring the Liberty Bell from Pennsylvania to the fair. Signed by children of all races, it was carried on the large reel seen here down Market Street to the Ferry Building. From there it was sent to Philadelphia.

Sir Thomas Lipton, center, surveys the Exposition site on November 5, 1912. Sir Thomas issued a challenge for a 23-meter yacht race to take place in 1915, but later dropped out to devote his time to war relief work. The yacht races were reduced to a Pacific Coast regatta.

FIRST LOAD OF LUMBER to be delivered to Panama-Pacific Exposition Grounds Furnished by SAN FRANCISCO LUMBER CO. hauled by FEDERAL 1½ TON TRUCK

PANAMA-PACIFIC EXPOSITION 1915 SAN FRANCISCO

ABOVE

March 8, 1912: A truck hauls the first load of lumber for the Exposition, which used over 100 million board feet of lumber. Most of the lumber was Douglas fir from Oregon and was delivered to the Exposition docks by steam schooners at a rate of 3.5 million board feet a week.

The Horticultural Palace under construction, with steamrollers in the foreground preparing the roads. This building was a huge bubble of glass 185 feet high and 152 feet in diameter. Two hundred tons of steel and 47,000 square feet of glass were used in the dome. All of the Exhibition buildings were coated with plaster made of a high-grade gypsum from Utah, to which were added pigments such as French ochre, raw umber, and Italian burnt sienna. Hemp was used in the plaster to simulate the veining and striation of travertine marble. ♦ **O**nly 12.16 acres of the 635 acres making up the fair site were owned by the Exposition Company. The rest was leased, to be returned to the original owners in its original condition. Most of the land was leased until June 1916, some until January 1917. This was the reason for the temporary nature of the buildings.

The Oregon Building nearing completion. Built entirely of Douglas fir, it was modeled after the Parthenon. Forty-eight logs made up the colonnade, each 5 to 6 1/2 feet in diameter and 42 feet tall, the maximum length that would fit on a railroad flatcar.

The Machinery Palace, styled after the Roman Baths of Caracalla. It was the largest wooden and steel building in the world. Inside over 250 exhibitors displayed more than 2,000 exhibits in two miles of aisles. Uncle Sam's entire Army and Navy could have fitted into this Palace with room to spare. Aviator Lincoln Beachey flew through the building before it was completed, in the first-ever indoor flight.

Groundbreaking for the California Building, with Exposition president C.C. Moore presiding. Mayor "Sunny Jim" Rolph is seated in the first row, second from left. Phoebe Hearst, president of the Woman's Board of the Exposition, is in the first row, second from the right. The Woman's Board members were the official hostesses of the Exposition and were in charge of entertainment and reception at the California Building.

Workmen color the light globes in gentle pastel colors. The lighting at the fair was designed by General Electric, under the supervision of W. D'Arcy Ryan. No light bulb was seen directly, except on the Zone. The ornamental lamps used to illuminate the exteriors of the buildings were screened from view by elaborate colored silk banners. Special effects were abundant; for example, on St. Patrick's Day everything was lit in emerald green. ♦ Indirect illumination was an innovation at the fair, and the architecture was enhanced at night by masked lamps flooding the walls and ornaments. The buildings became more beautiful with the varying intensities of the hidden lamps.

Lucia Mathews working on one of the murals she and her husband, Arthur, created for the fair. The Mathews were both celebrated artists and leaders of San Francisco Bohemia. They painted murals to be hung over the entrance to the Court of the Four Seasons, including *The Arts* and *The Victorious Spirit*. He was also a member of the International Jury of Awards at the PPIE. *The Arts* is on view in the lobby of the Mechanics Institute in San Francisco.

A work in progress, one of two murals by Frank Vincent du Mond. This one depicts the arrival of pioneers on the West Coast. Pictured are Father Serra, Bret Harte, William Keith, Grizzly Adams, and others. The murals were hung beneath the Arches of the Setting Sun and the Rising Sun in the Court of the Universe. *Pioneers Arriving in the West* may be seen in the Reading Room of the Main Library in San Francisco, and *Pioneers Leaving the East* is in the library's Reference Room.

A figure from *Nations of the East,* a dramatic sculpture that was placed on top of the Arch of the Rising Sun in the Court of the Universe. A large staff of highly skilled workmen was hired to turn out the thousands of sculptures and decorations for the fair. The work was done in huge warehouses near the Machinery Palace. All the statues were made of plaster and tinted to match or complement the buildings. Many of the artisans were later brought to Hollywood, where they created scenery for D. W. Griffith's monumental film, *Intolerance.* Griffith attended the fair and was astounded by the architecture and decoration.

The grounds of the
Exposition were enclosed
on the city side by what
was without a doubt the
most unusual fence in the
world. Designed by John
McLaren, chief of land-
scape gardening, it is best
described as a vertical
lawn, 30 feet high and
1,150 feet long. Planted
with *Mesembryanthemum
spectablis,* or ice plant, in
certain seasons it was
covered with delicate
pink blossoms.

The date of the fair in light bulbs on the tower of the Ferry Building at the foot of Market Street. An airplane flies overhead promoting the PPIE. ♦ **E**ach Sunday, starting about a year before the opening, people assembled on the fairgrounds for a charge of 25¢ to watch the progress of the fair. Lincoln Beachey entertained with his feats of daring. Often there were as many as 50,000 people in attendance.

Looking down Scott Street at the main entrance to the fair. McLaren's hedge is clearly visible.

Opening day at the Scott Street gates. The city was wide awake by 6 a.m. Every bell and whistle in the Fire Department and every automobile horn was blown. A fife and drum corps had been sent about the city to wake each part of town. Many people had already purchased opening day badges for 50¢ each, which entitled the wearer to enter the grounds. A parade formed at Van Ness and Broadway and stretched back 2-1/2 miles. Mayor James Rolph and Governor Hiram Johnson were at the head of the parade. Rolph was so excited that he started to run! ♦ At 10 a.m., over 150,000 people began to enter the Scott Street gates. A prayer was given, speeches were made, and a message was sent to President Wilson in Washington, D.C., from Exposition President Charles Moore in San Francisco. Wilson pressed a golden key that was attached by wire to the 835-foot aerial tower at Tuckerton, New Jersey, and radio waves were sent 3,000 miles to the top of the Tower of Jewels. At that point the main portal of the Machinery Palace swung open, and the Fountain of Energy began to flow. The fair was open!

Gatemen at the Scott Street entrance. The admission fees were adults 50¢; children under twelve, 25¢ (15¢ on Saturday and Monday); schoolchildren in groups of twenty, 5¢. Soldiers and sailors in uniform were admitted free. Visitors could also buy special ticket books with their photo on them, good for the duration of the fair. The fair opened at 10 a.m. on opening day. For the next 287 fair days it opened at 7 a.m. At blasts from the siren on the Machinery Palace, the Palace doors opened at 9 a.m. and closed at 6 p.m. The gates to the fair closed at 11 p.m.

The Fillmore Street entrance to the fair. Trolley service to the fair was outstanding. You could take an E (for Exposition) car to the Scott Street gates or get off at Fillmore Street if you wanted to go to the Zone first. In all there were eight entrances to the fairgrounds: the Presidio, Baker Street, the Yacht Harbor, a direct ferry slip, Laguna Street, Van Ness Avenue, Fillmore Street, and Scott Street.

The beautiful South Gardens. The Tower of Jewels and Avenue of Palms are on the left, and Festival Hall is straight ahead just beyond the Fountain of Energy. The gardens were in continuous bloom with daffodils, tulips, pansies, begonias, and dahlias, each in their turn.

A closer view of sculptor A. Stirling Calder's Fountain of Energy, the ornamental center of the South Gardens. Its center-piece is a fine sculpture of victorious youth joyously proclaiming the union of the Atlantic and the Pacific by the Panama Canal. Calder was the acting chief of sculpture at the fair. His son Alexander would become famous for his mobiles.

LEFT

A rainy day for the International Grand Prix Race. No. 19, Eddie Rickenbacker in his Maxwell racer, makes a left turn on Palm Avenue at the Palace of Varied Industries. Rickenbacker joined the Army Air Corps in 1917 and accompanied General Pershing to France, where he downed 26 enemy planes during the war.

LEFT

Winners of the 104-lap International Grand Prix Race. No. 9, Dario Resta in a Peugeot, won first prize, $3,000. He was an Italian-born English racer who completed the Grand Prix in 7 hours, 7 minutes, and 57 seconds. His average speed was a little over 56 mph on a wet track. No. 26, Howard Wilcox in a Stutz, won second prize, $2,000. No. 28, Hughie Hughes in Frank Young's Ono, won third prize, $1,500. No. 5, Gil Anderson in a Stutz, won fourth prize, $1,000.

RIGHT

The International Grand Prix Race, February 27, 1915. The race was 400 miles around a 3.9-mile course.

No. 6, E.E. Ruckstell, in a Mercer car. He was ahead for the first lap of the Vanderbilt Cup Race on March 6, but broke an axle and was forced out in the 72nd lap. The 77-lap, 300-mile race was shorter than the International Grand Prix. The cup was donated by W.K. Vanderbilt, Jr., and Mrs. Vanderbilt was in the grandstand with Governor Hiram Johnson and Mayor Rolph. The winner, Dario Resta, received the gold cup and $3,000.

LEFT

Barney Oldfield, right, with his trademark cigar and bandana, in his Maxwell car before the start of the Vanderbilt Cup. Oldfield was the most famous driver at the fair and drove car No. 1.

LEFT

Motion picture star Grace Darling, known for her daredevil antics, with Howard Wilcox in his Stutz racer.

Luther Burbank, center, is honored in the Palace of Horticulture. Mayor Rolph, on Burbank's right, gave praise to his magical creations. Fair decorator Charles Vogalsang, on his left, presented him a memorial bronze plaque. A horticulturalist, Burbank came to California in 1875. After he developed the Burbank potato, he bred many new varieties of plants, including berries, tomatoes, squash, the Santa Rosa plum, the Shasta daisy, the fire poppy. Burbank, who had an important display in the California Building, distributed thousands of packets of seeds to fairgoers.

One of the fair's best rest spots, near the Horticulture Palace. A battery of powerful lights made the dome of this breathtaking building glow like a giant opal at night.

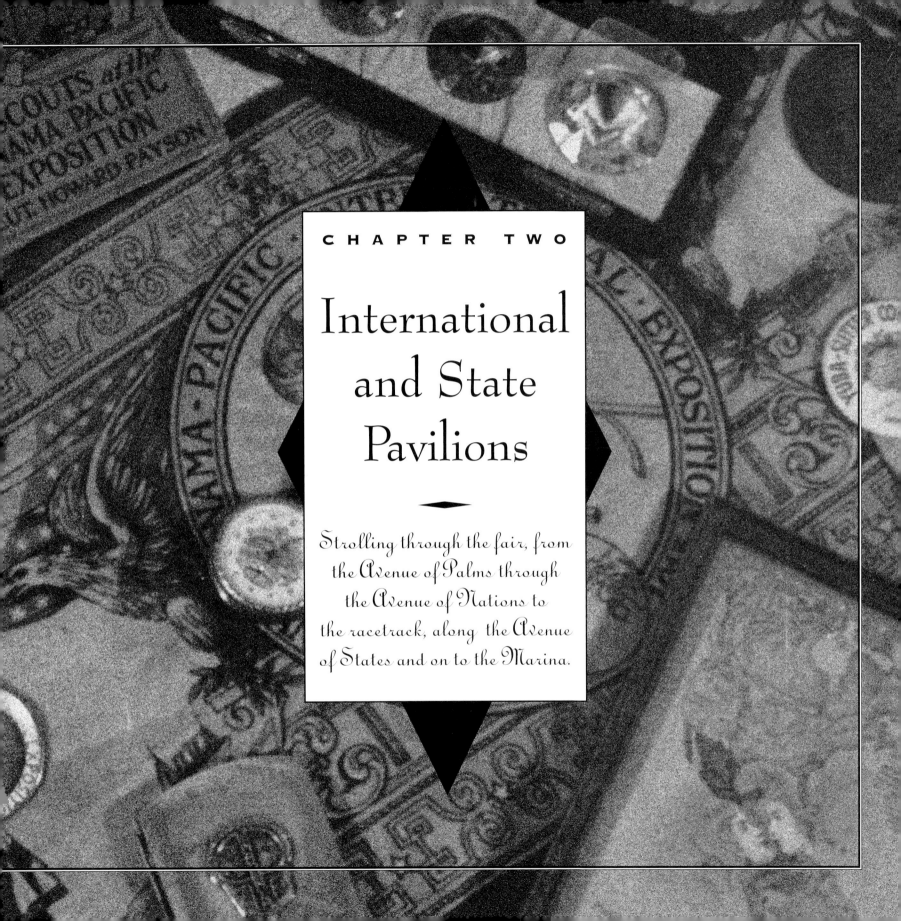

CHAPTER TWO

International and State Pavilions

—◆—

Strolling through the fair, from
the Avenue of Palms through
the Avenue of Nations to
the racetrack, along the Avenue
of States and on to the Marina.

Overlooking the Fine Arts Palace and Lagoon. The Japanese Pavilion, the French Pavilion, the Danish Pavilion (just to the right of the Fine Arts Colonnade), and the Cuban Pavilion (the tower with the flag directly behind the Fine Arts Palace) are clearly visible. Thirty-one foreign countries participated in the fair, and 21 built pavilions.

The Palace of Fine Arts, the beauty spot of the fairgrounds. The works of art displayed within the Palace and the grounds surrounding it attracted hundreds of thousands of fairgoers. The creation of architect Bernard Maybeck of Berkeley, the building inspired San Franciscans to save it from the beginning of the fair in 1915. The Palace *was* saved, and, although it stood in disrepair for many years, the dream of preservation came true in 1959 when philanthropist Walter Johnson gave $1 million to begin fundraising for restoration. (He ultimately gave much more.) It took years and many more dollars, but the Palace now stands in all its glory as the only original building on the fair site. (The Exploratorium and the Palace of Fine Arts Theatre are now popular permanent attractions in the building.) ♦ Showing his versatility, Maybeck also designed the House of Hoo Hoo for the Lumberman's Association. Located in the Forestry Court at the Exposition, it was made entirely of rough-barked tree trunks. The Exposition Livestock Buildings were also designed by Maybeck.

The Wave, by
Lorado Taft, on
the margin of the
Fine Arts Lagoon.

LEFT

Japanese dignitaries and President William Howard Taft at the fair on Japan Day, August 31, 1915. In February 1911, President Taft had invited foreign nations to participate in the PPIE. He came to the fair for Japan Day and gave a speech. That day was also the birthday of his Imperial Japanese Majesty Yoshihito. September 2 was declared to be Taft Day.

LEFT

Building guards in front of the French Pavilion, a copy of the Palais de la Légion d'honneur in France. Rodin's bronze figure *The Thinker* is in front of the building. Society matron and patron of the arts Alma Spreckels liked the French Pavilion so much that she had it reproduced for the Palace of the Legion of Honor Museum in San Francisco's Lincoln Park. She also became a patron of Auguste Rodin. The French Pavilion contained the largest exhibit area of any foreign nation's building, quite a feat considering that France was then at war in Europe.

RIGHT

An artist sketching by the Fine Arts Palace Lagoon. The beauty of the fair attracted artists from all over the globe. There was no charge to artists, but photographers had to buy a 25¢ camera license.

The Golden Pavilion, a copy of a Japanese temple. The Japanese occupied a large area in the fair. Rare Japanese gardens and two graceful teahouses fronted the Pavilion of Denmark and the southern entrance to the Fine Arts Palace. The gardens covered over three acres. Rocks—some weighing as much as three tons—25,000 square feet of turf, 1,300 trees, 4,400 small plants, and tons of small stones and gravel were brought from Japan. ♦ Japan was represented in other areas within the fairgrounds, including exhibits in the Palaces of Fine Arts, Education, Liberal Arts, Manufactures, Mines, and Transportation. Japan Beautiful was near the Zone, and a miniature landscape garden with dwarf shrubs, ponds of goldfish, and aquatic plants was in the Palace of Horticulture. The hospitality of the Japanese was a major contribution to the social life of the fair.

Teddy Roosevelt in front of the Argentine Building. As President, he had led the fight for the Panama Canal in 1903. On July 21, 1915, Roosevelt gave a speech at the fair entitled "Peace and War."

The Canadian Pavilion, one of the largest and most impressive on the grounds. Its extravagant displays depicted the agriculture, scenic beauty, wildlife, mining, and products of Canada, filling over 75,000 feet of exhibit space. A masterpiece diorama showed Canada's tremendous wheat belt, with two miniature trains moving grain across the oceanlike prairies. The Pavilion also featured a pond with a colony of beavers. Their activities were a delight to thousands of children.

RIGHT

The Siam Pavilion. Built in Siam, it was then taken apart and reconstructed on site at the Exposition. Every detail was personally examined by the Crown Prince before the Pavilion was shipped to California. It was considered one of the most picturesque buildings at the fair.

BELOW

A crowd in front of the Guatemala Pavilion. Inside, Hurtada's Marimba Band entertained regularly. Guatemala was the first country to accept the invitation to exhibit at the Fair, 18 days after President Taft's proclamation was issued.

The Italian Pavilion, a whole village of seven beautiful buildings, surrounded by flowered courts adorned with fountains and replicas of Italian art treasures. It cost nearly $200,000 to build, one of the largest sums spent by a foreign country at the fair. In the foreground on the right is a wicker basket chair called an Electriquette, which ran on a storage battery. For a rental price of $1 per hour, this was an enjoyable way to see the fair.

The pavilion of Portugal, which was filled with photos of Portuguese architecture as well as historical objects. Most of the international buildings provided rest and refreshment for their visitors.

Washington State Livestock Day. Sixty-five acres were set aside for livestock at the fair.

ABOVE

The San Francisco
SPCA, always on call to
help animals day or night,
picks up a mule by the
Livestock Arena.

RIGHT

The Overfair Railway, a
rapid means of transporting
footsore visitors along the
scenic shores of the
Exposition grounds. The
concession belonged to

inventor L.M. MacDermot of Oakland. The trains were one
third the size of a standard locomotive, the first of this size to
be constructed. The 24-foot-long cars seated 16 passengers
and carried them 2-1/2 miles. Six stations were located along
the Marina out to the racetrack. The fare was 10¢. Today,
three of the beautifully restored trains are on a private estate
in Los Gatos, California, and another is in the Railroad
Museum in Sacramento.

The Ohio Building, a replica of the Ohio State Capitol at Columbus. The scene of many receptions and social affairs, the rotunda contained busts of former Presidents from Ohio: McKinley, Grant, Harrison, Hayes, Garfield, and Taft.

Overlooking the western portion of the Exposition from the edge of the Presidio. The foreign pavilions are in the foreground, with the state buildings against the Bay. The Fine Arts Palace and the Astoria flagpole are on the right. This 214-foot flagpole, next to the Oregon Building, was the largest ever made from a single tree.

Four young women from Washington State dressed as mermaids join Miss Spokane to promote Salmon Day at the fair. Five thousand cans of salmon were given away on that day.

Pioneer Ezra Meeker. In 1852 Meeker traveled across the country over the Oregon Trail; in 1906 and 1907 he retraced his route. He sold books and pamphlets on his travels in this booth.

The Oregon Building, representing the Parthenon. Inside were exhibits of natural resources, a lecture hall, and a picture gallery. The art room displayed woodwork, stained-glass windows, myrtlewood furniture, and rugs made by Oregon artists.

The Liberty Bell arrives on July 16, 1915. The parade moved up Grove (pictured) to Van Ness and on to the Scott Street entrance to the fair. After a lavish ceremony, the bell was moved to the Pennsylvania Building.

The Pennsylvania Building. Each state building was the headquarters for visitors from that state. For the first time in any exposition, most of the state buildings had motion picture theaters with movies explaining the resources and wealth of each state. The film *Fatty and Mabel at the Fair*, starring Fatty Arbuckle and Mabel Normand, was made to advertise the fair.

Children posing with the Liberty Bell. On November 10, 1915, a farewell tribute was given to the bell, and on November 11, it began its journey home to Philadelphia, traveling 16,000 miles through 24 states.

The California Building. The largest state building ever erected at any exposition in history, it cost more than $2 million to construct and covered five acres. The architecture was that of an old Spanish mission with seven bell towers. Inside the building was a spacious reception hall and ballroom, plus exhibits from each of the state's 58 counties.

The tranquil lagoon in the Court of the Four Seasons. The Court was 340 feet across and shaped like an octagon. Through the archway you can see the Palace of Fine Arts.

Looking out a window of the California Building. The ship is the battleship *Oregon,* which stayed in the Bay until the fair closed on December 4. In this room visitors could rest, read, and send postcards home.

These beauty contest finalists in front of the Palace of Fine Arts were part of Cadillac Day at the Exposition. Owners of Cadillac cars from all over the country came to town. Hundreds of models—from the old-time one-cylinder machine to the modern eight—could be seen. The event was organized by Van Ness Avenue Cadillac agency owner Don Lee.

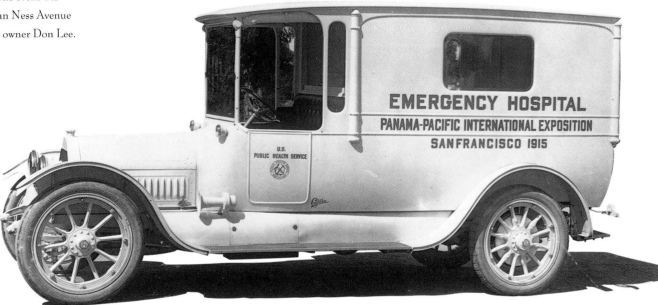

RIGHT

One of the two Cadillac ambulances belonging to an emergency hospital located in the Service Building. The hospital was equipped with a full corps of surgeons, nurses, and attendants as well as all the latest appliances known to medical science. Cases treated ranged from fatigue and fainting spells to dislocations and fractures from falls.

Lincoln Beachey and a fan in his airplane. A 26-year-old native of San Francisco, Beachey was the most famous aviator in the world. He was regarded as "death proof" because he persistently defied death with his stunt flying.

Lincoln Beachey waving good-bye to the crowd as he takes off in his monoplane on March 14, 1915. In a newspaper story on March 13, Beachey had expressed concern about the safety of his experimental airplane. He was right to be concerned, as this flight was to be his last; he would fall to his death while flying over the Bay. He was looping the loop at a height of 2,000 feet and had made three turns when the fatal accident occurred. His flying machine collapsed, and he fell from a height of 500 feet. The machine sank into the mud with Beachey strapped in.

Beachey's biplane, on a Packard truck en route to the Palace of Transportation.

LEFT

A powwow of Blackfoot Indians, staged by the Great Northern Railway and Glacier National Park. This was the first performance of medicine lodge rites outside a reservation. The Blackfeet adopted two San Francisco children into the tribe during the ceremony.

ABOVE RIGHT

Art Smith and friends on Glacier National Park Day at the fair. Smith was the fearless aviator chosen to take Lincoln Beachey's place.

BELOW RIGHT

Native Americans of the Blackfoot tribe arrive at the Exposition from Montana.

Three views of Art Smith and his biplane. Smith cut new and fancy capers every week. His daytime flights were so full of thrills that some who witnessed them were overcome with spells of dizziness. His night stunts defied the imagination. He looped and side dipped and set off fireworks from his plane. He then looped and somersaulted through the fireworks back to earth. He sometimes appeared above the landing spot enveloped in a cloud of smoke (caused by an exploding can of gunpowder), then wobbled back to earth like a wounded butterfly. Often he extinguished his searchlight, leaving the thousands on the earth below to guess his whereabouts. Then he would suddenly switch the light on again and flash into view over the Zone or beyond the Tower of Jewels, like a star gone mad.

Art Smith in his baby racer, the Comet. The fair had a Baby Vanderbilt Cup Race and a miniature Grand Prix Race in which the Comet was featured.

Admiral Thomas Benton Howard (in plumed hat), commander in chief of the Pacific fleet, accompanies U.S. Vice President Thomas Marshall on a visit to the battleship *Oregon*.

A view of the fairgrounds from the battleship *Oregon*. Built by the Union Iron Works in San Francisco, the *Oregon* steamed to Cuba in 1898 on a 14,000-mile journey to take part in the Spanish American War. This journey focused attention on the need for a quicker route from coast to coast. Arriving at the Exposition in late 1914, she stayed until the fair closed, anchored 400 yards off the Marina. Thousands of people visited her.

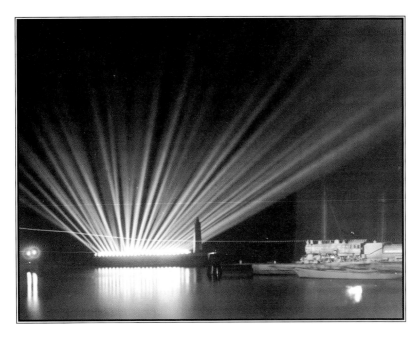

The Scintillator sent 48 beams of light in seven colors across the sky above the Exposition. The beams were projected through steam created by a stationary locomotive on a platform in the Bay.

A Christian Home Church baptism in the Bay during the PPIE.

Japanese visitors take part in the Oriental Kite Flying Contest on the Marina Green, May 15.

A replica of the San Francisco Ferry Building sails by the fair on San Francisco Harbor Day, October 23.

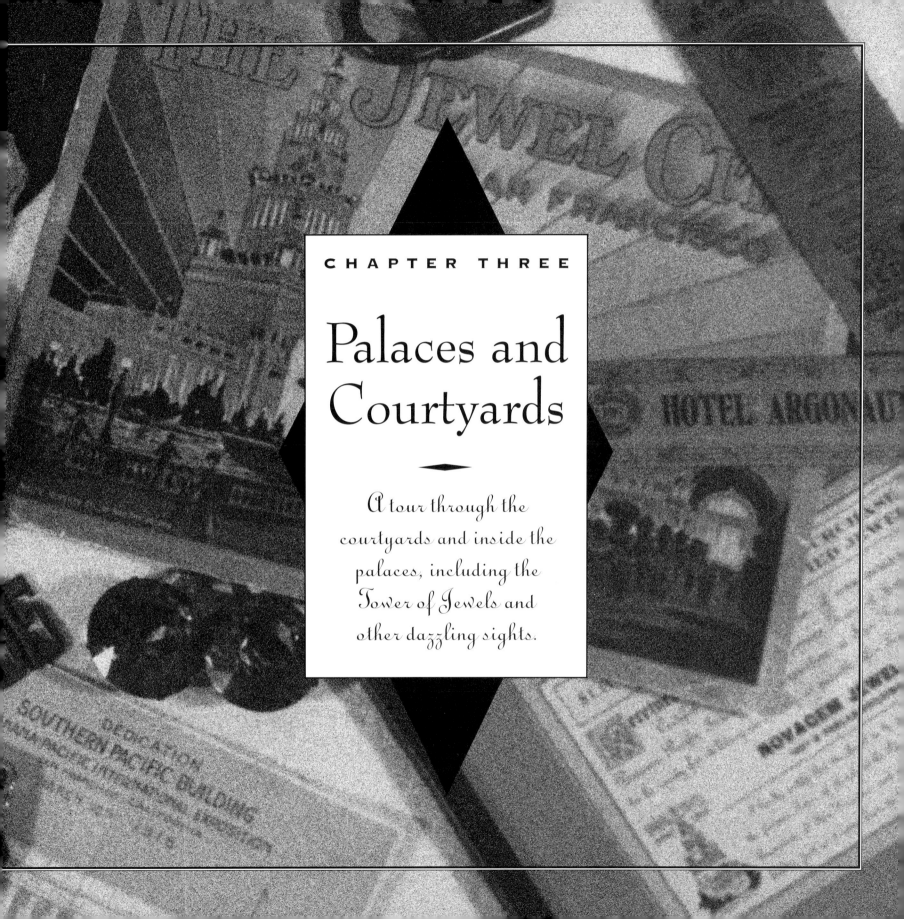

CHAPTER THREE

Palaces and Courtyards

◆

*A tour through the
courtyards and inside the
palaces, including the
Tower of Jewels and
other dazzling sights.*

A pyramid of 57 varieties of canned and bottled Heinz foods reaches high into the air. Free Heinz pickle pins were given out as souvenirs. H.J. Heinz had introduced his pickle pin at the Columbian Exposition in Chicago in 1892; they were also given away at the 1939 fair on Treasure Island in San Francisco.

The Sun-Maid Raisin exhibit in the Palace of Agriculture and Food Products. Also in the Palace were the exhibits of 14 nations including, among other things, a fish hatchery, an operating tobacco factory, a flour mill turning out 90 barrels of flour a day, and a model kitchen. Visitors could breakfast with the nations here. Natives in costumes served the traditional breads and pastries of their country.

The MJB Coffee exhibit at the Epicuria in the Food Products Building. Cakes, sandwiches, and scones filled with butter and jam were sold for 5¢ each to accompany cups of coffee.

LEFT

The Food Products Club booth. This club sponsored the wedding of one of its most popular members during the fair. Many people left presents for her in this booth, and all fairgoers were invited to the wedding on November 17. After the ceremony, 10,000 boxes of wedding cake slices were given away!

TOP

A pie-eating contest on Food Products Day.

BOTTOM

Women promoting some of the products exhibited in the Food Products Palace.

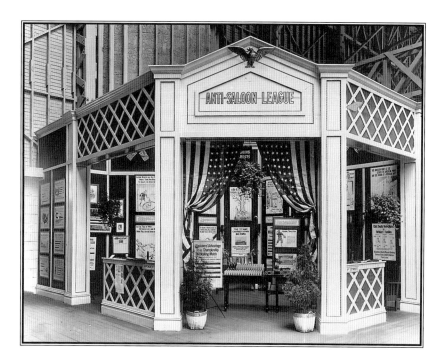

The Anti-Saloon
League booth. The
League attempted to
stop the consumption of
alcohol in the United
States. Prohibition
would eventually be
enacted in 1920 and
repealed in 1933.

The suffragette booth, sponsored by the Congressional Union for
Women's Suffrage. This was the first exposition to have suffragettes.
Susan B. Anthony's portrait hung in the booth (she was called the
Mother of Suffrage). Thousands of people signed a petition here to pass
the Suffrage Amendment, which was before Congress. California
women had been given the vote in 1911, but it was not until 1920,
with the passing of the Nineteenth Amendment, that all American
women were given that right.

Dr. Maria Montessori, an expert on child psychology and education, in feathered hat, with a demonstration class in the Palace of Education. The committee to bring Dr. Montessori to the Exposition included Dr. David Starr Jordan, president of the National Education Association and chancellor of Stanford University, and Margaret Wilson, daughter of President Wilson. Schools for the blind and the deaf were also located in this building.

The $100,000 typewriter, "an exact reproduction of the machine you will eventually buy." Seventeen hundred and twenty-eight times larger than the Standard Underwood, it weighed 14 tons. News stories were typed daily on this machine at the Underwood Exhibit in the Palace of Liberal Arts. The message in the photo announces the sinking of the *Lusitania*.

The 20-inch Equatorial Telescope, a central exhibit in the Palace of Liberal Arts. One of the largest refracting telescopes in the world, it weighed ten tons. It was made for Chabot Observatory in Oakland, California, and is now in use there.

Souvenir booths at the Exposition. Everyone wanted a momento of his or her visit to the fair. Fairgoers could buy badges, pennants, silk scarves, jewelry, pillows, view books, spoons, postcards, copies of jewels from the Tower of Jewels, and just about anything else anyone could imagine.

The 435-foot-tall
Tower of Jewels, the
central structure of the
Exposition, and the
great gate to the fair.
Decorated with
102,000 highly polished
cut-glass "novagems"
that swayed in the
breeze, the Tower was by
night ethereal and by
day lively and sparkling.
The jewels were made of
Bohemian glass in a
variety of colors: ruby,
emerald, white, pink,
purple, and aquamarine.

Roy La Pearle singing from the top of the Tower of Jewels. His powerful baritone voice floated out over the fairgrounds every day at noon.

A close-up view of the top of the Tower of Jewels.

The *End of the Trail,* by sculptor James Earle Fraser, in the Court of the Palms. This 25-foot-tall sculpture was one of the most popular and poignant works of art at the fair. The dying Indian astride his exhausted horse depicted the Native American's failed battle against encroaching civilization. The statue now resides in the Cowboy Hall of Fame in Oklahoma City, Oklahoma.

John Philip Sousa and his 65-piece band on the grandstand in the Court of the Universe. An extremely popular attraction, Sousa performed at the fair for nine weeks.

PALACES AND COURTYARDS

Panorama of the fair.

William Jennings Bryan at the fair on July 5. As secretary
of state, Bryan had been instrumental in inviting foreign
nations to participate in the Exposition. His speech here,
on the subject of peace, drew over 121,000 people. Edwin
Markham, the author of the famous poem "The Man with
the Hoe," is seated directly behind him.

A gaily decorated car promotes Adams Pepsin Gum.

A float in the Army and Navy Men's Clubhouse Day parade on April 8. The Clubhouse was located on the Avenue of Nations, near the Canadian Pavilion.

MARE ISLAND NAVY YARD VALLEJO, CAL.

ADAMS PEPSIN GUM

In the Court of the Universe, looking east at the triumphal Arch of the Rising Sun, crowned with the sculpture *Nations of the East*. A glimpse of the Palace of Machinery can be seen through the Arch. Immediately in front of the Arch is the Fountain of the Rising Sun, with the Fountain of the Setting Sun in the middle distance. The beautiful Star Maidens, by A. Stirling Calder, graced the whole upper balustrade of the Court of the Universe. Each Star Maiden wore sparkling jewels in her headdress like those on the Tower of Jewels.

RIGHT

Sculptor A. Stirling Calder completing a Star Maiden.

ABOVE

One of two Beniamino Bufano medallions, each of which was fixed on a Roman arch on either side of the Court of the Universe. Bufano was one of the fair's many talented sculptors. This medallion symbolizes art guiding the child to nature for inspiration.

LEFT

The Court of Abundance, designed by Louis Christian Mullgardt of San Francisco. One of the most original courts of the Exposition and perhaps the most beautiful. The walls were pink, with a deep terra-cotta tone, and the vaults above were blue. The arches were a smoked ivory color. In the corridor were murals by Frank Brangwyn representing Earth, Air, Fire, and Water. Sculptor Leo Lentelli's *Aquatic Maids* are in the foreground. Lentelli's sculpture studio was located at 1761 Union Street

LEFT

Bicycles and their motorized counterparts on exhibit in the Palace of Transportation. The Excelsior Auto Cycle Company displayed its products next to those of Harley-Davidson, then the fastest motorcycle in the world.

TOP

Lotta Crabtree, the city's darling in Gold Rush days, arrives at the Exposition for Lotta Day. Thousands of people greeted her. Lotta's singing and dancing had captured the heart of a young San Francisco during the 1860s.

BOTTOM

One of the myriad of conveyances that appeared at the fair on Transportation Day.

BELOW **RIGHT**

The Gillette Safety Razor Company booth, one of the most unusual at the fair. Giant razors hold up the pavilion.

A booth promoting one of the many health products presented at the fair.

A giant desk telephone of wood and iron on display in the Palace of Manufactures, part of the Western Electric Company exhibition of electrical goods and appliances. The first transcontinental telephone call was made by Alexander Graham Bell from New York City to the fair, before it opened, on January 25. Transcontinental telephone calls, then considered a remarkable development, were made daily at the fair.

The City of Paris Drygoods Company exhibit in the Industrial Arts Palace. These figures, created by French artist Pierre Imans, wear gowns created by Madame Valerio of the City of Paris and decorated with stones resembling opals, sapphires, and emeralds. The setting is a reproduction of the gardens of Versailles.

RIGHT

One of the fair's several tobacco booths. Cuban cigars were well represented at the Exposition.

LEFT

A booth of C. G. Conn's musical instruments. The first Sousaphone was created by Conn for John Philip Sousa.

RIGHT

A refreshment counter for weary fairgoers.

LEFT

The Marshmallow Creme booth in the Palace of Food Products.

The Southern Pacific Building, which gave visitors easy access to transportation and other information. Exposition guests used this building to receive and send mail and as a resting spot during excursions about the grounds.

Visitors walk through California Big Trees in the "Glade" exhibit inside the Southern Pacific Building. Other replicas of famous scenes along SP routes included Lake Tahoe, Yosemite, Riverside's orange groves, and Mount Shasta.

The PPIE fire department. A high-pressure water system was installed for the Exposition grounds, and three engine houses were built. The exhibit buildings had automatic sprinkling systems and were further protected by concrete fire walls on the sides facing the courts.

One of the 20 white Fadgl Auto Trains that quietly conveyed thousands of visitors over the grounds. R. B. Fageol, an Oakland auto dealer, invented auto trains. The fare was 5¢ to 10¢, depending on the destination.

The conveyor system in Machinery Hall
transports the products of fair exhibitors.

The Inside Inn, the only hotel within the fairgrounds. Containing over 1,100 rooms, the Inn also featured a florist, a candy shop, a drugstore, a barber shop, an express office, and news and novelty stands. The steam-heated rooms were generous in size, and most had private baths. Rates ranged from $1 to $5 per night. The Grill Restaurant, which had a special room for women dining alone, was very popular. A special entrance to the Expo was provided at the Inn, and admission to the fair was included in the price of the rooms. Many celebrities, including Henry Ford, stayed here.

A luncheon in honor of Thomas Edison, seated to the right of C. C. Moore, in the center of photo under sea horses, and Henry Ford, seated on Moore's left, on October 21 in the California Building. Edison received a Certificate of Award for the storage battery that he had perfected and which was on display at the fair. Because of Edison's deficient hearing, Ford acted as his escort to the Expo.

Henry Ford, on left wearing a dark suit, poses with a Model T engine. Ford was only one of many famous visitors to the fair, who included Buffalo Bill Cody, Billy Sunday, Al Jolson, "Diamond Jim" Brady, Harry Lauder, Helen Keller, Francis X. Bushman, Charlie Chaplin, Harry Houdini, and Madame Schumann-Heink.

The Ford assembly line in the Palace of Transportation. This exhibit turned out one car every ten minutes for three hours each afternoon except Sunday, and always drew a large crowd. Forty-four hundred cars were produced at the fair.

A portion of the Westinghouse exhibit in the
Transportation Palace, showing a giant Pennsylvania
Railroad electric locomotive. With 4,000 horsepower and
weighing 156 tons, this was one of 33 locomotives that
operated out of Pennsylvania Station in New York City,
carrying 12 million passengers annually.

Festival Hall, the musical center of the PPIE. Situated on the east side of the South Gardens, it had a seating capacity of 3,500 and was said to have excellent acoustics. The second-largest pipe organ in America, it was built to order for the Hall and transported across the country on eight freight cars. At the close of the Exposition it was installed permanently in Civic Auditorium.

La Loie Fuller, "The Mistress of Light," with the cast of "A Thousand and One Nights." This petite native of Illinois had captivated audiences throughout Europe with her modern dance interpretations. At the fair she was accompanied by the PPIE orchestra.

Camille Saint-Saëns with the Exposition orchestra. Saint-Saëns wrote "Hail California!," the official Exposition symphony, for this orchestra.

Assistant Secretary of the Navy Franklin D. Roosevelt (third from left) at the fairgrounds with C.C. Moore (to his left) and entourage.

Crowds at the fair on San Francisco Day, November 2. This celebration was grander than anything held at the Expo to that date. Three hundred and fifty thousand people were in attendance, the biggest crowd ever assembled on the Pacific Coast.

Tellers with the receipts from San Francisco Day: $125,000 in admission receipts and $86,000 in concession sales. San Francisco Day boosted admission to over 16 million people. By closing day, December 4, over 18 million people had passed through the entrance gates.

The IXL Company wagon, filled with boxes of its products.

The Red Seal Lye Company car with a giant facsimile of a can of lye.

CHAPTER FOUR

The Zone

Visiting the amusement,
education and concession
attractions on the eastern
side of the fairgrounds.

The Panama Canal on the Zone, a detailed reproduction of the great waterway. This exhibit covered five acres with the topography of the country accurately laid out in accordance with the original plans of the Panama Canal Zone. A panorama of the country and the oceans gave a bird's-eye view of 5,000 square miles of land and water. Miniature steamers and railroad trains ran to and fro. A moving platform with seats carried spectators around the exhibit, while a duplex telephone receiver at each seat conveyed information to the passengers. Admission was 50¢ for the half-hour ride.

The official Panama Canal souvenir booth, which included paperweights filled with soil from the famous Culebra Cut and plaques made from the cocobolo wood used for railroad ties across the Isthmus of Panama.

The entrance to the Zone, with the Ghirardelli Chocolate Parlor on the left.

ABOVE

Children and adults on the Zone. By means of a carefully worked-out system, Exposition guards were able to locate and bring together separated parents and children with little confusion. Eight hundred efficient guards were on duty. The Exposition also provided day care for children from three months to ten years of age.

ABOVE

The Frankfurter Inn, source of a newly popular snack. You could eat in any language at the PPIE, sampling German, Japanese, French, Italian, and Turkish fare among others. At the forty-niners' camp on the Zone, you could eat off tin plates amid all the trappings of a mining camp.

RIGHT

A cigar concession, with the entrance to the Bowls of Joy on the left. The Bowls of Joy, a hair-raising ride around the inner surface of two cones, was so dangerous it was shut down twice.

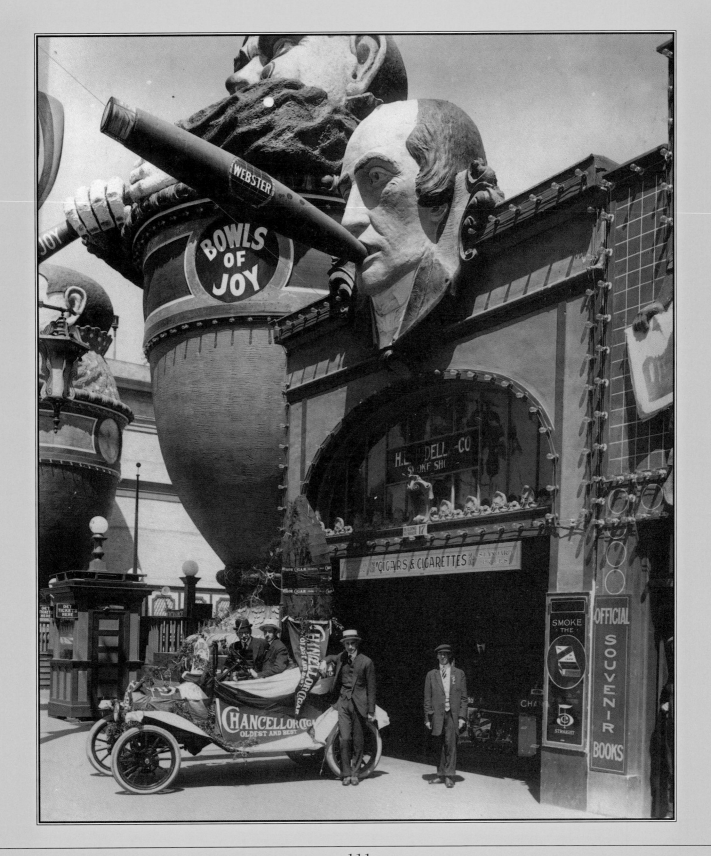

View from the Bowls of Joy. Across the way is the Jester's Palace,
a funhouse full of crooked mirrors and moving staircases.

The Creation, on the Zone. Inside, the first chapter of the Book of Genesis was depicted in tableaux sequences with gorgeous colors and beautiful electric effects. Admission was 25¢.

A parade advertising watches passes by the Souvenir Watch Palace, presided over by a giant Uncle Sam. The Palace did an enormous business, as watches were considered a great souvenir. Many of these same watches still function today.

Looff's Carousel, the finest one ever built on the Coast. Looff was a famous carousel maker of the time, and this ride was specially constructed to be in harmony with the Jewel City. The horses, camels, goats, and other animals were all covered with paste gems. A ride cost 10¢.

Suggestive attractions along the Zone included "the kick" (a dance) at the Streets of Cairo, the hula in the Hawaiian Village, and Stella for a dime. Stella was a detailed painting of a woman that was so lifelike she seemed to undulate. She was considered quite shocking for the time.

Captain, the Educated Horse, the smartest horse living. He played songs on bells, added, subtracted, and matched colors. Admission was 10¢.

The Ostrich Farm Exhibit was an exotic attraction. The sight of this strange bird drew large numbers of patrons.

A Native American grandmother and granddaughter at the 101 Ranch on the Zone. This Wild West show featured cowboys, cowgirls, Indians, and a stagecoach. The 101 Ranch also led a colorful parade around the fairgrounds daily.

A Navajo girl at the Grand Canyon on the Zone. The Grand Canyon of Arizona was beautifully reproduced on five acres by the Santa Fe Railroad. Deluxe coaches carried the visitor on a 20-minute trip from El Tovar Hotel through the Canyon. Carloads of sandstone, cactus, sage, pine, and adobe brick were brought in from the desert for this $250,000 project. Pueblo Indians were brought from their Southwestern reservation to live in a village above the Grand Canyon on the Zone, where they made pottery for sale. Fred Harvey of restaurant fame had a fine collection of Indian blankets and rugs for display and sale here.

Dancers in the Samoan Village on the Exposition grounds. Exhibitions of native dancing were given here, as were demonstrations of craftspeople making jewelry from tortoiseshell and sharks' teeth. The Samoans arrived on the S. S. *Matsonia* after a stormy 4,500-mile trip across the Pacific. The 120-foot gilded Buddha in Japan Beautiful, another exhibit, is visible in the background.

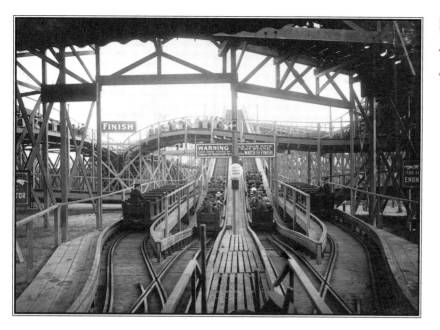

The Safety Racer, an
exciting ride on the Zone.

This woven mesh of ropes
suspended above the ground
was a favorite spot for young
people on the Zone.

The Scenic Railway,
a one-mile ride.

Fred Thompson's Toyland GU (the initials stood for "grown up") featured scenes from children's nursery rhymes blown up to gigantic proportions. Those who entered had the sense of being very small. ◆ **A** giant suffragette (far left) marks the exhibit's entrance. Many women were offended by this creation.

In the Giant's Kitchen at Toyland GU

The Infant Incubators exhibit on the Zone. Created to educate the general public, this exhibit demonstrated that with proper treatment babies with weak constitutions could be made strong and healthy. To lend color to the enterprise, five storks were brought from Budapest to live in the hospital gardens.

Presented by the Union Pacific Railroad, the stucco and burlap mountains of Yellowstone National Park tower above the fences at the east end of the Zone. The Old Faithful Inn was the scene of many Exposition banquets and entertainments. An orchestra played there daily.

The Aeroscope, carrying a car of passengers to an elevation of 285 feet. The bird's-eye view from the ride was spectacular, especially at night. Built by bridge engineer Joseph Strauss, who perfected the counter-balanced drawbridge, the Aeroscope looked like a drawbridge sitting on a counterweight. Strauss built 400 bridges, including the Golden Gate.

Night illumination of the Zone.

After the Lights Went Out

RIGHT

Although it had seemed as if this dream would never end, on the balmy night of December 4, 1915, the lights went out for the last time. The lights faded slowly while taps was played by a bugler high atop the Tower of Jewels. The word *Finis* appeared on the gallery of the Tower. Fireworks were discharged, and Art Smith glided into the velvet sky in his airplane, turning over and over and trailing wreaths of fire. The last beam of light was directed at the famous statue *Descending Night* and went out exactly at midnight. At 4 a.m. people still refused to believe it was over. But it was.

LEFT

The southwest corner of the Court of the Universe is toppled, while the Adventurous Bowman on the Column of Progress temporarily remains standing. The Tower of Jewels has already been removed. Built for a cost of $413,000, it was sold to a demolition firm for $9,000. Individual jewels were sold for $1 to souvenir hunters.

LEFT

One of the Italian Towers at the entrance to the Court of Palms and the Court of Flowers after being dynamited.

It is truly the end of the trail as this statue is moved from its place in front of the Court of Palms.

The demolition of the Zone. Uncle Sam on the Souvenir Watch Palace no longer looks festive as the area is reduced to rubble.

Part of the salvage of the fair, waiting to be sold or dispersed. Some statues, such as the *Nations of the East* and *Nations of the West,* could not be salvaged and were broken into thousands of pieces when the arches were dynamited. The work of wrecking structures and restoring the land was completed by early 1917. Over $900,000 in income was realized from salvage efforts. Everything that wasn't sold was destroyed. The Victor Talking Machine Company exhibit was moved to San Rafael, where it became the home of the Improvement Club.

The Ohio Building floating down the Bay on two barges, eventually almost ramming the Dumbarton Bridge in the process. It was purchased for $1,000 and became the Babylon Club, an impressive night spot in San Mateo County. Used as an airplane parts company through World War II, it was burned down to make room for an asphalt plant in October 1956.

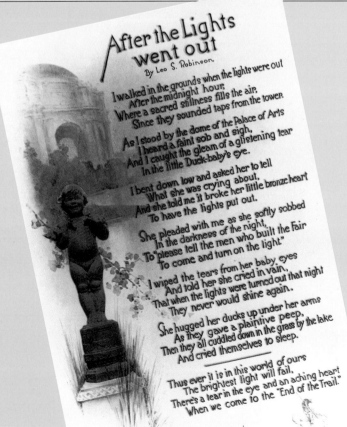

After the Lights went out
By Leo S. Robinson

I walked in the grounds when the lights were out
    After the midnight hour,
Where a sacred stillness fills the air,
    Since they sounded taps from the tower.

As I stood by the dome of the Palace of Arts
    I heard a faint sob and sigh,
And I caught the gleam of a glistening tear
    In the little Duck-baby's eye.

I bent down low and asked her to tell
    What she was crying about,
And she told me it broke her little bronze heart
    To have the lights put out.

She pleaded with me as she softly sobbed
    In the darkness of the night,
To "please tell the men who built the Fair
    To come and turn on the light."

I wiped the tears from her baby eyes
    And told her she cried in vain,
That when the lights were turned out that night
    They never would shine again.

She hugged her ducks up under her arms
    As they gave a plaintive peep,
Then they all cuddled down in the grass by the lake
    And cried themselves to sleep.

Thus ever it is in this world of ours
    The brightest light will fail,
There's a tear in the eye and an aching heart
    When we come to the "End of the Trail."

The fair site is desolate as
the land is being returned
to its pre-Exposition state.
Only the Palace of
Fine Arts, the Argentine
Pavilion, the California
Building, and the Column
of Progress remain.